NATIVE
AMERICAN
NATIONS

Nez Perce

F.A. BIRD

Checkerboard
Library

An Imprint of Abdo Publishing
abdobooks.com

ABDOBOOKS.COM

Published by Abdo Publishing, a division of ABDO, PO Box 398166, Minneapolis, Minnesota 55439.
Copyright © 2022 by Abdo Consulting Group, Inc. International copyrights reserved in all countries.
No part of this book may be reproduced in any form without written permission from the publisher.
Checkerboard Library™ is a trademark and logo of Abdo Publishing.

Printed in the United States of America, North Mankato, Minnesota
102021
012022

THIS BOOK CONTAINS
RECYCLED MATERIALS

Design and Production: Mighty Media, Inc.
Editor: Liz Salzmann
Cover Photograph: ELAINE THOMPSON/AP Images
Interior Photographs: Ad_hominem/Shutterstock Images, p. 7; August Frank/AP Images, p. 29; Edward
    S. Curtis/Library of Congress, p. 13; Everett Collection/Shutterstock Images, pp. 15, 19, 27; Gerard
    Stolk/Flickr, p. 9; Hanjo Hellmann/Shutterstock Images, p. 5; Jimmy Emerson/Flickr, p. 25; Library of
    Congress, p. 23; mariait/Shutterstock Images, p. 17; Martin Prochazkacz/Shutterstock Images, p. 21;
    topseller/Shutterstock Images, p. 11

Library of Congress Control Number: 2021942970

Publisher's Cataloging-in-Publication Data
Names: Bird, F.A., author.
Title: Nez Perce / by F.A. Bird
Description: Minneapolis, Minnesota : Abdo Publishing, 2022 | Series: Native American nations | Includes
    online resources and index.
Identifiers: ISBN 9781532197215 (lib. bdg.) | ISBN 9781098219345 (ebook)
Subjects: LCSH: Nez Percé Indians--Juvenile literature. | Indians of North America--Juvenile literature. |
    Indigenous peoples--Social life and customs--Juvenile literature. | Cultural anthropology--Juvenile
    literature.
Classification: DDC 973.0497--dc23

Contents

CHAPTER 1

Homelands

The Nez Perce (ness purse) lived on the Columbia Plateau where present-day Oregon, Washington, and Idaho come together. This region is also known as the Pacific Northwest.

The Pacific Northwest is cold in the winter. Large snowdrifts made travel difficult and dangerous. During the winter, the Nez Perce moved down from the mountains into the warmer canyons.

The Nez Perce homelands included around 17 million acres (6.9 million ha). They stretched west toward the Cascade Mountains and east toward the Rocky Mountains. The Nez Perce believe that they have lived in this region since the beginning of time. They call themselves the *Nimi'ipu* (nee-me-poo). It means "the people." The *Nimi'ipu* speak a **Sahaptin** language.

The Pacific Northwest has mountains, canyons, forests, and swift streams and rivers.

CHAPTER 2

Society

The Nez Perce were the largest Native American tribe in the Pacific Northwest. They numbered about 6,000 in 1800. They were divided among more than 70 villages. The villages were often named after the river the **band** settled next to.

Each band had a "headman," or chief. This headman was an **elder**. Sometimes, the headman was a **medicine man**. He healed the sick and performed ceremonies.

The Nez Perce believed all their people should help make important decisions. They selected three or four members to sit on the village council. The council worked to do what was best for the people.

THE NEZ PERCE HOMELANDS

WASHINGTON

Columbia River

Cascade Mountains

Columbia Plateau

OREGON

IDAHO

Rocky

Mountains

MONTANA

NORTH DAKOTA

MINNESOTA

WYOMING

SOUTH DAKOTA

WISCONSIN

MICHIGAN

NEW YORK

MAINE

VERMONT

NEW HAMPSHIRE

MASSACHUSETTS

RHODE ISLAND

CONNECTICUT

NEW JERSEY

PENNSYLVANIA

NEVADA

UTAH

COLORADO

NEBRASKA

IOWA

ILLINOIS

INDIANA

OHIO

WEST VIRGINIA

VIRGINIA

DELAWARE

MARYLAND

WASHINGTON, DC

CALIFORNIA

KANSAS

MISSOURI

KENTUCKY

TENNESSEE

NORTH CAROLINA

ARIZONA

NEW MEXICO

OKLAHOMA

ARKANSAS

SOUTH CAROLINA

MISSISSIPPI

ALABAMA

GEORGIA

TEXAS

LOUISIANA

FLORIDA

ALASKA

HAWAII

N W O E S

THE NEZ PERCE HOMELANDS

CHAPTER 3

Homes

The Nez Perce lived in tepees, longhouses, and pit houses. In the 1700s, the Shoshoni introduced the Nez Perce to the horse. Horses helped the Nez Perce travel greater distances. They could trade with the Native Americans of the **Great Plains**. This activity introduced the Nez Perce to the tepee.

Longhouses were good winter homes. Each had several fire pits and **smoke holes**. The fires kept the entire home warm. The sides had many doors that allowed the families to come and go.

The Nez Perce built pit houses by digging a round hole that was five feet (1.5 m) deep. Then, a frame was built over the hole to support the roof and walls. This frame was covered with woven reed mats. Ladders helped people get in and out of the pit house.

Tepees were made of 12 wooden poles. These poles formed a cone-shaped frame. The frame was covered with buffalo hides that were sewn together.

CHAPTER 4

Food

Salmon was an important food for the Nez Perce. They used spears, lines and hooks, fiber-woven traps, and nets to catch the fish. Fishing season ran from spring until fall. Some fish were eaten fresh. Others were dried for winter use.

In the summer, the women gathered berries. Flowers were eaten fresh and dried for the winter. The Nez Perce mixed fruits, meat, and fat. This dried mixture was eaten in the winter and when traveling. The women also went to the prairies in search of food. They used sticks to dig up bitterroot, wild carrot, wild potato, and camas root.

The Nez Perce hunted deer, elk, bear, mountain goat, buffalo, and pronghorn antelope with bows and arrows. They also trapped rabbits, squirrels, and birds.

The Nez Perce fished for salmon in the fresh waters of the Snake, Salmon, and Clearwater Rivers of the Pacific Northwest.

CHAPTER 5

Clothing

Nez Perce men wore shirts, **breechcloths**, leggings, gloves, and moccasins. The clothes were made of **tanned** deer or elk skins.

Shirt sleeves had long **fringe** along their undersides. The seams and hems had shorter fringe. Shirts were also decorated with porcupine **quills**. Sometimes, the fringe was quilled too.

Women wore long buckskin dresses, knee-length moccasins, leggings, and woven hats. The dresses hung from the shoulders to the ankles. They were gathered at the waist with a belt.

Long fringe hung from the undersides and hems of the sleeves. The dresses were decorated with porcupine quills, elk teeth, and tusk shells. This long, tube-like shell was also worn as jewelry. Knee-length moccasins were decorated with porcupine quills.

Nez Perce men wore their hair loose or in braids. Each cut his hair above the eyes, so it stood high and fell a little to the side.

CHAPTER 6

Crafts

The Nez Perce are famous for their weaving, **quilling, and beadwork.** Women wove baskets used for gathering berries and roots. These baskets were also used to store food and hold water.

Quill workers put quillwork on leggings, **cradleboard** coverings, moccasins, and dresses. A quill worker used her mouth and teeth to soften and flatten each quill. Before the quill dried and became hard, it was carefully sewn into place.

Quill workers used **geometric** shapes to decorate clothing. The women colored their quills with dyes from berries, trees, and minerals.

Men wove fishing nets from plant fibers. They made bows from ash, willow wood, or the horn of a bighorn sheep.

Nez Perce women wove rounded, cone-shaped hats. They crafted the hats from hemp, grass, and cedar root fibers.

CHAPTER 7

Family

Men married at about 14 years old. Women married even younger. Their families arranged the marriages. A number of families often lived in one house. If a child was orphaned, another family could care for him or her.

The women cared for the home. They also gathered food, cooked, made baskets, and decorated the family clothing. The men hunted, fished, cared for the horses, and cut firewood. They also set up the pit houses and longhouses.

Families often traveled together to hunt buffalo. They went to the prairies east of Nez Perce homelands. Sometimes, hunting trips lasted for a year or more.

The Nez Perce are famous for their Appaloosas. These horses were valuable trade items. Appaloosas are still bred today.

CHAPTER 8

Children

Newborn children spent most of their time on wooden **cradleboards**. The babies were bundled in soft furs. Cradleboards hold babies tightly. This makes them feel safe.

Mothers and grandmothers taught the older children to be quiet and respectful. Grandmothers spent much time with children. They told them stories. These stories taught the children Nez Perce history and lessons about life.

The children helped the women pick berries and gather roots. The Nez Perce believed that children learned best by helping their parents. Girls learned how to **quill**, make clothing, care for the babies, and prepare food. The men taught boys how to hunt and fish. They also learned to take care of and ride their horses.

The Nez Perce cradleboard has a rounded top and a narrow bottom.

CHAPTER 9

Traditions

The Nez Perce have a creation story. Before humans existed, a giant monster swallowed many animals. Coyote wanted to help them. Coyote asked the Great Spirit for courage and wisdom.

The Great Spirit reminded Coyote of his guardian spirit, the grapevine. Then, Coyote knew what to do. He tied one end of a grapevine around his middle. He tied the other end to a tree. Coyote hid a knife in his mouth. He went up to the monster. It swallowed Coyote whole.

When Coyote reached the monster's heart, he used the knife to cut it out. The monster fell dead with its mouth wide open. Coyote and the other animals ran out. The Great Spirit told Coyote to make good use of the monster. Coyote cut up the body. Each piece created a new tribe of people. Then, Coyote squeezed the blood from the heart. From this blood, the Great Spirit created the Nez Perce.

Many Nez Perce stories feature Coyote.

CHAPTER 10

War

The Nez Perce only went to war to protect their land and people. In 1855, the US government wanted to open Nez Perce land to white settlers. The Nez Perce agreed to a treaty. It allowed them to keep 10,000 square miles (25,900 sq km) of their homeland.

In 1860, gold was discovered on Nez Perce land. The US government wanted the Nez Perce to give most of their land to the settlers and move to a **reservation**. Some Nez Perce **bands** signed the treaty. But the Wallowa band refused.

In May 1877, the Nez Perce War began. Five Nez Perce bands fought the US Army. For three months, the Nez Perce retreated from Idaho through Montana. But finally, many of the Nez Perce surrendered in the Bear Paw Mountains of Montana.

Nez Perce warriors often rode their horses in battle.

CHAPTER 11

Contact with Europeans

The Nez Perce first met Europeans on September 20, 1805. That's when the Lewis and Clark expedition arrived in their lands.

In 1804, the US government hired Meriwether Lewis and William Clark to map much of the land acquired in the **Louisiana Purchase**. Part of this land included the Nez Perce homelands of the Pacific Northwest.

The Nez Perce welcomed Lewis and Clark into their homes. They gave them food and supplies. Lewis and Clark told the Nez Perce of their goal to reach the Pacific Ocean. The Nez Perce knew how to get to the ocean.

The Nez Perce guided Lewis and Clark to the Columbia River. The river would take them to the Pacific Ocean. The expedition reached the ocean in November 1805.

A statue of the Nez Perce greeting Lewis and Clark stands at the Capitol building in Boise, Idaho.

CHAPTER 12

Young Chief Joseph

Young Chief Joseph (Heinmot Tooyalakekt) was born around the 1830s. He led the Wallamwatkin **band** of the Nez Perce.

In 1877, the US government ordered Young Chief Joseph and his people to move to a **reservation** in the Idaho Territory. Young Chief Joseph refused the order. Fights over land led to war the same year. The Nez Perce won many battles against the US Army. But Young Chief Joseph knew his people could not win the war.

Young Chief Joseph decided to retreat to Canada. He led his people across the Rocky Mountains and into Montana. By then, many Nez Perce were tired and ill. So, they made camp in the Bear Paw Mountains. But the US Army found the camp. On October 5, 1877, Young Chief Joseph surrendered.

Young Chief Joseph was the son of the great chief whose Nez Perce name was Tu-ya-kas-kas.

CHAPTER 13

The Nez Perce Today

As of 2011, there were 3,500 members of the Nez Perce Nation. Many of them live on the Nez Perce **Reservation** in Idaho. There are also Nez Perce on the Colville Reservation in Nespelem, Washington. Some Nez Perce also live in cities and towns across the United States.

Part of the traditional Nez Perce homelands in Oregon has been turned into the Eagle Cap Wilderness. No roads have been built there. The land looks like it did when the Nez Perce called it home.

The Nez Perce have a committee style of government. Tribal members elect people every three years. There are nine members of the Nez Perce Tribal Executive Committee.

Each year, the Nez Perce celebrate their **culture** during the Chief Lookingglass **Powwow**. It is held every August at the Nez Perce Reservation.

In 2021, members of the Nez Perce nation celebrated the renaming of historic Nez Perce artifacts purchased back from the Ohio Historical Society.

Glossary

band—a number of persons acting together; a subgroup of a tribe.

breechcloth—a piece of cloth, usually worn by men. It wraps between the legs and around the waist.

cradleboard—a decorated flat board with a wooden band at the top that protects the baby's head.

culture—the customs, arts, and tools of a nation or people at a certain time.

elder—a person having authority because of age or experience.

fringe—a border or trim made of threads or cords, either loose or tied together in small bunches.

geometric—made up of straight lines, circles, and other simple shapes.

Great Plains—pastureland east of the Rocky Mountains in the United States and Canada.

Louisiana Purchase—the land the United States purchased from France in 1803, extending from the Mississippi River to the Rocky Mountains and from Canada to the Gulf of Mexico.

medicine man—a spiritual leader of a tribe or nation.

powwow—a ceremony of Native Americans, usually involving feasts, dancing, and performances.

quill—a large, stiff feather or a sharp spine. To decorate something with quills is called quilling.

reservation—a piece of land set aside by the government for Native Americans to live on.

Sahaptin—a family of languages spoken by the closely related tribes that lived in the area where Washington, Oregon, and Idaho meet.

smoke hole—an opening in the roof of a longhouse to allow smoke to go out.

tanned—having been made into leather by being soaked in a special liquid.

ONLINE RESOURCES

Booklinks
NONFICTION NETWORK
FREE! ONLINE NONFICTION RESOURCES

To learn more about the Nez Perce, please visit **abdobooklinks.com** or scan this QR code. These links are routinely monitored and updated to provide the most current information available.

Index